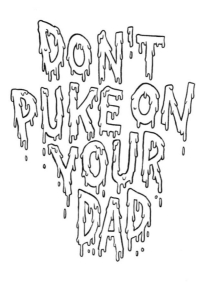

A YEAR IN THE LIFE OF A NEW FATHER

BY TOBY MORRIS

Beatnik Publishing

PO Box 8276, Symonds Street, Auckland 1150, New Zealand.
www.beatnikpublishing.com

First published in 2013 by Beatnik Publishing

Text & Illustrations: ©Toby Morris 2013
Toby Morris: www.xtotlworldwide.com
Editor: Brynne Clark
Photography: ©Sonya Nagels 2013
with the exception of the traditional dutch family portrait which was
taken by Foto de Boer, a tourist photography studio in Volendam, the Netherlands

Printed and bound in China.

ISBN 978-0-9922493-5-9

For Max, obviously.

A baby? Me?

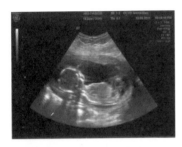

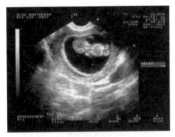

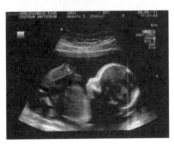

IT GROWS!

You get a lot of advice when you're about to have your first baby. Women get all the practical stuff — nappies, nap times, nipple shields — but from men to other men most of it is something like 'there is no way to describe what you're about to go through'.

We found out we were having a baby in the middle of a holiday. We were living in Amsterdam but were back home in New Zealand for a series of summer weddings. We'd been trying for a while, but not in a particularly focussed or organised kind of way, so even though it was something we'd been wanting to do, it still took us by surprise somewhat when it actually happened. All of a sudden it felt like things were about to get very different. This was really happening.

What would it be like? Would we be able to handle it? Would I be able to provide for a family? Would my social life go completely out the window? Would my friends still hang out with me? Is this when I'd finally feel like

DUE-DATE DOODLE

I'd grown up? I didn't know what to expect, apart from expecting that everything would change. A new life. One night early on in the pregnancy I arrived home drunk to find the entry to our tiny apartment blocked by a hulking great new pram.

I owned a pram! Me!

But as my Dad said to me, you get nine months to get used to the idea. Nine months to drag yourself through all the early stages of panic, doubt, nervousness, through to false confidence, ending up in real confidence and massive excitement.

Because you start to see that belly grow. And you start to feel it kick and you begin to fill your house with tiny hats and socks and you start talking about names and soon, without even realising it, you've shifted your thoughts from yourself and devoted them all to this amazing unknown being that is slowly introducing itself. All your fears about your own ability to cope, or provide, or maintain your lifestyle are suddenly irrelevant and the wonder begins to grow: who this new character is who is going to enter your life? This person whose school plays you will attend, whose scraped knee you'll nurse, whose wedding you'll probably pay for. That is currently the size of an orange. And is currently inside your girlfriend's belly.

You realise that it isn't about you.

You suddenly learn that most things aren't.

TOBYMORRIS
Grey Lynn, Auckland, New Zealand.

MEET
MAX BUCKLEY MORRIS
BORN 30TH SEPT. 2011
MBM
EIGHT THIRTY A.M.
AT SINT LUCAS ANDREAS, AMST
Mother & Child:
HEALTHY
(FATHER: PROUD)
IN NO HURRY
Weighing in at
3.94
KILOS
TINY FINGERS
TINY TOES

MAX BUCKLEY MORRIS

Chapter One
"wow"

30 SEPT. 2011

OLD MAN HANDS

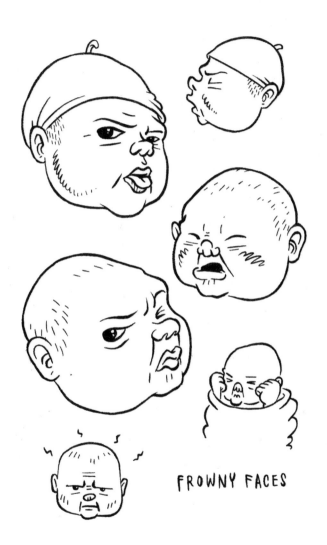

FROWNY FACES

These first days are a blur. Feeding, sleeping, crying, changing. Feeding, sleeping, crying, changing. It's a whirlpool that never seems to stop.

I'm losing all sense of time. There is no night, there is no day, it all blurs into one.

We're filled with a mixture of excitement, disbelief that we're actually allowed home with this new creature, and a kind of cautious awe. Mix that with delirium from days of broken sleep, and all order is gone. We're grabbing sleep when we can — an hour here, or three hours there - anything more than five hours is a real treat. One moment I realised I had an hour's window to sleep and I literally ran to the bed to soak up every second.

You're fueled by the excitement; it's a rush, a whirlwind. For Sonya, it's the 24 hour feedings, which take so long and have to be done so often. I'm caught in a loop of nappy changes, loads of washing, dishes, cups of tea, and lots of walking around in circles trying to get Max to sleep when Sonya crashes.

The world becomes small. We're barely leaving our tiny little apartment, but still it seems like a whole new place. Everything else seems unimportant. Our gaze turns inwards as we stare in wonder at the whirlpool dance.

Us and Max, together: feeding, sleeping, crying, changing.

LIGHT
STREAMING
IN, SONYA
LOOKS SO
BEAUTIFUL

FIRST ALL BLACKS GAME,
WORLD CUP QUARTERFINAL,
VS ARGENTINA WITH OMA

BUCKET BATH
-TOTAL BLISS

POST-FEED, MILK DRUNK.

After a few weeks, the whirlwind slows down, you rub your eyes and begin to stumble back into the real world. Like a butterfly in reverse, you climb out of your cocoon as a slow and squishy caterpillar.

After weeks of being so gentle at home, so tender and careful, I'm finding it a shock to re-enter society again. Riding my bike into town to meet my mates for a beer, I suddenly feel like everyone else is riding so fast, driving so aggressively. People are crossing the road without looking, kids are playing near the edge of the canal. People are yelling, cars are honking horns.

Slow down, I feel like shouting! Don't you know Max is trying to sleep!? Haven't you seen how soft the back of his head is?

THE PARENT
PICK-UP

GRUMPY MAX
DOESN'T LIKE
HIS CUTE-SUIT

SONYA AND MAX
NAP IN THE
MORNING LIGHT

MAX AS MAX

WORK HALLOWEEN
PARTY

SKYPE WITH NEW ZEALAND FAMILY...

ONE MONTH CHECK-IN

Hair mostly growing on sides and back of head. Old man style.

Eyes starting to track and focus. First tears coming.

Sleeping well, still likes a good cry in the evenings

Little belly growing fast

Pants tucked firmly into socks.

Favourite album: Bon Iver

5.14kg
56cm

Chapter Two

Everything's changed.

November 2011

SOMETIMES MAX
SLEEPING SILENTLY
FREAKS ME OUT

I've never been afraid of Death. But the thought of Max dying? Heart stoppingly terrifying.

I'd be lying if I said I didn't think about it now. Everyone talks about the good things about having a baby, but what no-one tells you is that there is a lot of fear too.
Life and Death. This is the serious stuff.

All of a sudden Death is something that crosses my mind fairly often, and it scares me so much. Max is so fragile, so tiny and vulnerable. Defenseless. It's such a miracle that he is here, alive and breathing, that it seems too easy to believe that he might not be. That one day he won't be. I don't want to think about it, but I have these terrible moments where I can't help but worry.

It's the silence that gets me. When he's fast asleep and the house is silent I stand there in the dark, trying to think positive thoughts, holding my hand in front of his face to feel his breath.

SMILES

FIRST NIGHT OUT. LUCY & RACHEL BABYSIT.
SONYA CAN'T STOP CHECKING HER PHONE.

For a while there are two distinct worlds:
1. Home. 2. The outside world.

At home is this new, intense situation: three people trying to
get into a routine and enjoying the whirlwind of sleep and spew.
While at work, and with my friends, I'm trying to get along like
normal, do my thing, business as usual. Act like everything hasn't
changed.

Slowly, these worlds are expanding and combining again. As we
get our routine down at home, we're starting to enjoy a degree
of control. The whirlpool is slowing down, and we're confident
enough to leave the nest.

Bringing the baby out of the house in a social sense is a big
step. As much as I wish they weren't, things are different now
with my mates, especially the ones who aren't parents. I found
it really hard to talk about all the things that were going on
beyond a surface level, and it was hard for them to understand
my new priorities. I couldn't drop everything and come out
for a beer like before, not to mention the physical logistics of
leaving the house. Packing the nappy bag for all contingencies is
a dark art. It's hard work to pull off a stress free catch-up.

But like most things you just have to start doing it and assume
you can only get better. My quickfire pub-toilet nappy change
techniques are improving, that's for sure.

JUST QUIETLY...
SLOWLY...
GENTLY...
SAY IT SOFTLY, DON'T SCARE IT...
Calm
is settling in.
(SSSSH)
x

I SPOKE TOO SOON ABOUT THE CALM DIDN'T I?

SHOWERTIME

UNCLE DAN
WALKS LAPS
OF THE
LOUNGE

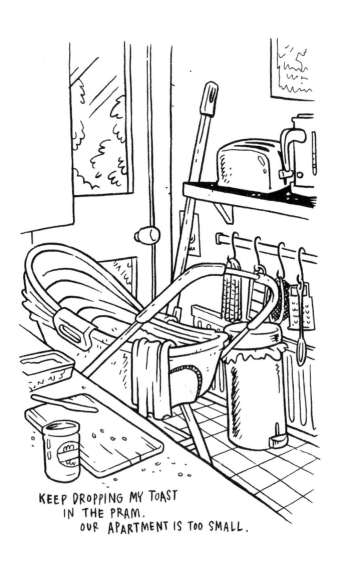

KEEP DROPPING MY TOAST
IN THE PRAM.
OUR APARTMENT IS TOO SMALL.

HOMESICK.

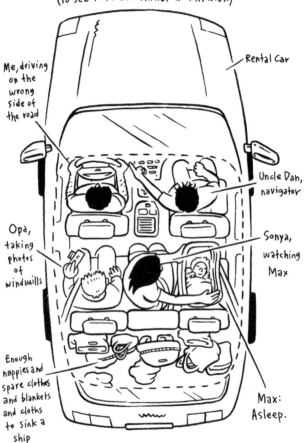

1AM. WORKING,
WITH MAX

SO STRONG

SONYA SAYS
ALL THE LADIES AT MOTHER-BABY YOGA
ARE BLOWN AWAY BY HOW STRONG MAX IS.

I FEEL AMAZINGLY PROUD OF THAT.

EVERY
THING
CHANGED

life's harder but better

YEP.

Chapter Three

GETTING BIGGER

December 2011

When I first found out we were having a baby, my boss Eric Quennoy was great. I consider him something of a mentor, so to get his advice was valuable.

What stuck with me was a story he told: "Having a baby is about losing self-indulgence. When my wife and I used to be hungover, it'd be an all day affair. 'Oh, I can't move, I need to stay in bed. Oh, let's cancel that thing we were going to do and watch a cheesy movie. Let's get takeaways for dinner. Poor us.'"

But once you have a baby, this has to end. The baby doesn't care that you didn't get dinner before you went out, that you mixed wine, beer and some weird shots, that you stayed out too late. The morning is the morning to the baby. Where's the milk?

But guess what? You can get up. You have to, and you do. And yeah, you've got a headache, but life goes on.

FAVOURITE POSE #72
THE WISE OLD MAN

BABY
SWIMMING CLASS.

MUMS IN THE POOL,
DADS FILMING FROM THE SIDES.

TRADITIONAL AFTER-BATH JOKE

I'M TIRED.
I'M STRESSED.
I HAVE A MILLION
THING ON MY MIND.

BUT WHEN MAX SMILES

NOTHING
MATTERS.

WHEN I HAVE A NIGHT AWAY FROM MAX,
I SPEND IT TALKING ABOUT MAX.
— WORK CHRISTMAS PARTY

Damn! I didn't want to be that guy! Listening
to people talk about their children is only
5% more interesting than listening to people
talk about their dreams. Which is not at all.
Especially if you haven't got kids.
And especially if the kids aren't there.
And you're supposed to be having a party.

But have you seen my kid?

Did someone say kid?

Did you just ask why I was away from work
recently?

No?

Sorry, I can't really hear you!

His name is Max!

GRANNY AND G-POP
(AKA MY PARENTS)
ARRIVE FOR CHRISTMAS.

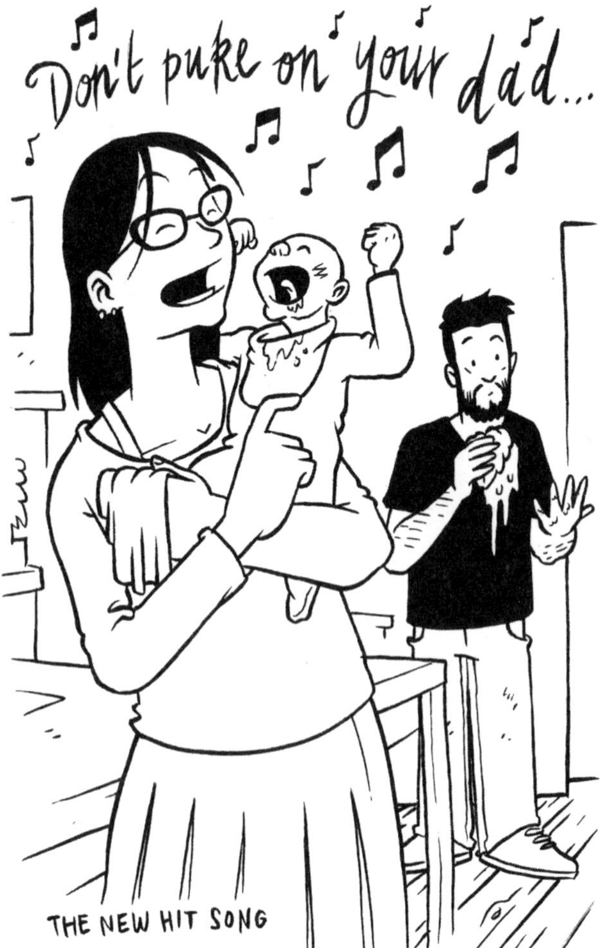
Don't puke on your dad...
THE NEW HIT SONG

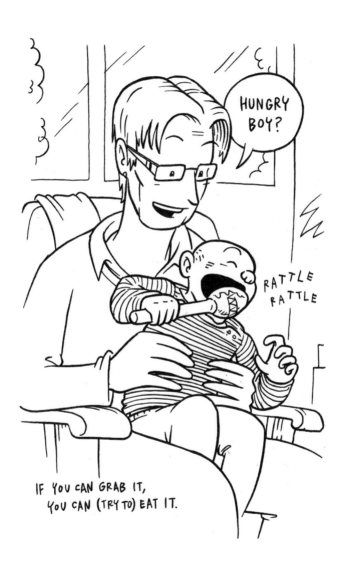

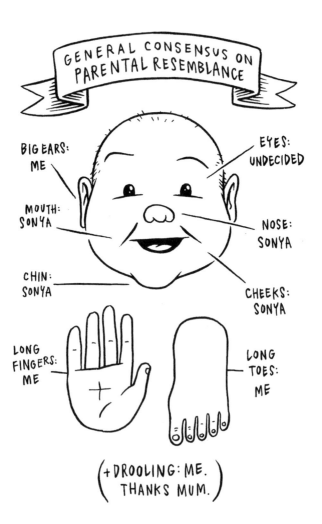

Everyone does it: the tallying up of recognisable features, the comparing of noses, hairlines, ear lobes, finger lengths. Keeping score.

Why do we care? Is it just pride? You want to see yourself in your child, but at times I couldn't help but get competitive about it. From the day Max was born, everyone said he looked like Sonya, or her brother Dan, and I have to admit it was a strange feeling. "It's my beard!" I'd say. "If he had a beard you'd say he looked like me!"

It's not something you should take personally, but you find yourself taking it on board. Luckily my parents cleared it up. All the cute things about him – that was Sonya. All the other bits – the drooling, his big ears, his finger toes? That was apparently me.

I can take that, finger toes are cool. Honestly.

13 MONTH OLD WHIRLWIND
TOBY COMES AROUND WITH
DARIO AND MARIEKEN.

FEELS LIKE LOOKING TEN
MONTHS INTO A VERY
ACTIVE FUTURE.

3 MONTHS

Much more aware, smiling and responding to play.

Learning to grab, using his hands deliberately.

More hair!

Tries to eat anything that comes near his mouth.

(A little slobbery...)

Favourite album:
Twerps –
Through the day

6.4 kg
63 cm

Chapter Four

CHAOS

January 2012

NEW YEARS EVE:
POOR LITTLE FELLA
IS STUNNED BY THE
FIREWORKS

SOMETIMES I MISS PARTYING,
SOMETIMES I DON'T.

SITTING AND CHATTING
ON THE COUCH

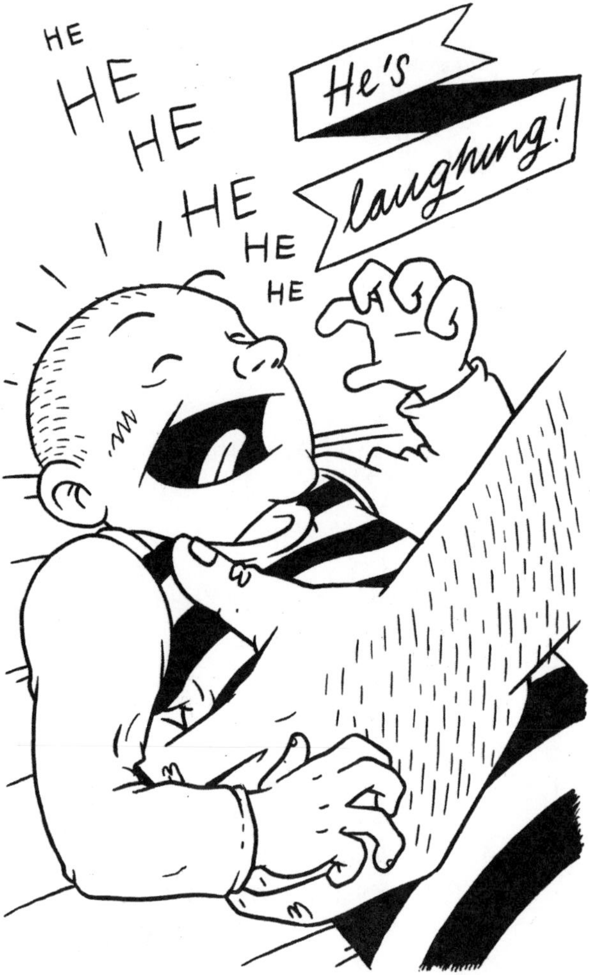
HE
HE
HE
HE
HE
HE
He's laughing!

It's needless to say, but somehow never gets said: having a baby has seriously altered our relationship. We've gone from two to three. From boyfriend and girlfriend to a family. That's a big change.

During the pregnancy we spent a lot of time staying home and talking about the future. What kind of parents we wanted to be, what type of lives we wanted to lead. Quality time.

Then the baby came and we were off on this insane new trip. Side by side, but often too wrapped up in what we were doing individually to really notice where we were going together. It's a huge test of a relationship – you're tired, strung out and seeing each other at your worst daily. We both had new and sometimes confusing roles to play and no time to stop and talk or really think. You're thrust into being a family on the run, adjusting as you go, at a time when you're more tired and emotionally muddled than you've ever been.

But something else amazing and intangible happened. Sonya isn't just my girlfriend anymore, she is the mother of my child. She's family. There's an intense new bond that feels secure and solid. There's a new trust and confidence. We're in it together. We're not mucking around anymore. It feels good.

In all that madness, it's easy to forget something else too – we just don't get the time or space to go out just the two of us, as a couple. On our tenth anniversary, we went to dinner at Marius. It was my all time favourite dining experience.

EVERYONE MISSES MY
PARENTS ALREADY

THINGS HAVE TO CHANGE

MY LONG HOURS WITH WORK AND THE EXHIBITION AREN'T JUST GOING TO BURN ME OUT, THEY'RE GOING TO BURN SONYA OUT TOO. REALLY IS TIME TO SLOW DOWN A LITTLE BIT.

Life has changed, and I have to adapt. I'm a workaholic, so I've found it very hard to step back.

My day job is as an advertising creative, a job that often means long and unpredictable hours, because it doesn't have a finite end to the day. When I was a dishwasher, once I had washed all of the dishes, I went home. When I was a magazine designer, once I'd designed the magazine, I was done. The task ended. But when the task is to 'think about success', or 'what does 'here' mean?", then you can think about it for 8 hours, or you can think about it for 80. They also give you a lot of free alcohol, so in busy times it's easy to let the job take over your life. And I make it worse by coming home late in the evenings and staying up to draw. That's what I've done for the past few years.

It's really hard to make a conscious change, but I'm realising that I have to. My choices don't just affect me anymore: Sonya has been carrying more than her share of the parenting and it's starting to wear her down. Nothing is more important than family, and it's easy to say that, but I need to do something about it. It's not just about me anymore it's about two people I love more than mobile phones, or football boots, or a certain Dutch beer brand. Time to go home and reset my lifestyle.

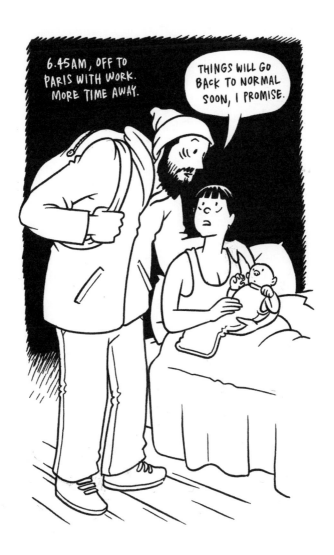

PROUD DAD AT
THE SHOW OPENING

Chapter Five

WINTER

February 2012

YOUTUBE EDUCATION

When Max has trouble sleeping, my go to technique is simple - hold him on my chest, walk in circles and sing *Twinkle Twinkle Little Star*. Nothing works better, and believe me I've tried a million other things. It's great to know you've got a trick that works, but seriously, you try walking in a tiny circle singing those same six lines over and over in a pitch black room for anything more than about ten minutes. Strange things start to happen in your mind.

But here's a great fact - *Twinkle Twinkle*, *Baa Baa Black Sheep* and the *Alphabet Song* are all pretty much the same song. To keep my brain from totally melting I like to pull out some remixes when I'm getting close to losing it.

Try this:
Twinkle twinkle little star
Yes sir, yes sir three bags full
Up above the world so high
One for the little boy who lives down the lane
Twinkle twinkle little star
Yes sir, yes sir three bags full

or expert mode:
Twinkle twinkle little star
H I J K L M N O P
One for the master, one for the dame,
Like a diamond in the sky
Now I know my A B C's
Yes sir, yes sir three bags full

NEW GAME:
PULLING OFF YOUR
SOCKS

Dudes don't let dudes baby talk. Right?

One thing that I found really hard to get used to is talking with the baby in public. At home it's easy: you can be as dumb or as cutesy as you like. But when you're around anyone else it's a different deal. Chatting away about whatever stupid thing comes into your head is so natural at home, but so hard when you know strangers are listening. And I think this is even harder for men.

In truth, I don't really talk baby talk at home. I'm trying to make a conscious effort to talk to him like a man, to treat him with respect. Still, it kind of ends up being more like talking to him like a baby man. I may not be doing a cutesy baby voice but the things I end up saying to him are pretty ridiculous. It's half about entertaining and stimulating the baby, and half about keeping yourself from going totally nuts.

It's natural and I'm sure very normal, but in front of anyone else my flow just dries up. I can't help but feel self conscious. I'm a quiet person in public usually - talking on the phone on a silent bus fills me with dread. Even around other parents, I find it tough to let myself relax, to let my guard down. As a man it's hard to show a softer side sometimes.

FIRST NIGHT AWAY
FROM HOME -
THREE IN THE BED

Chapter Six

Packing Up

March 2012

LITTLE CHARMER
AT JAIME'S BIRTHDAY
LUNCH

I'm in a happy, long-term relationship, so I probably shouldn't say this... But damn, hanging around with a baby is an incredible way to get to talk with beautiful women.

It's crazy but true: gorgeous girls will flock to you with a cute baby in your arms. They'll laugh and smile and be generally adorable because they're in full gush mode and pretty much nothing you say will distract them from being very happy and very cute. Let me say that again - beautiful women will approach you and talk to you in a friendly way. It's unbelievable. I feel like I should lend Max to some of my single mates from time to time.

And I'm not just fishing for a babysitter here.

OUR LITTLE DUTCHMAN:
MAX GETS HIS NETHERLANDS
PASSPORT (KIWI ONE IS IN THE MAIL)

MEN'S REACTIONS WHEN I'M OUT
WALKING THE PRAM BY MYSELF...

...AND WOMEN'S.

TEETHING:
YOU WANT TO
FIX IT, BUT
YOU CAN'T.

I'VE FINISHED
WORK NOW.

TWO WEEKS TO PACK
UP AND GET READY
FOR THE MOVE.

THERE'S A LOT
TO ORGANISE,

BUT FOR THE FIRST
TIME SINCE THOSE
EARLY WEEKS
I GET TO SPEND
DAYS WITH MAX.

MY FIRST
IMPRESSION?

THERE'S A LOT
OF WALKING
THE PRAM
INVOLVED.

It's so fun to watch your baby grow. The development process is like a crazy, niche soap opera that you get totally sucked into and no one except you, your partner and possibly your parents understands. Every little thing is a big deal to you. Tiny little differences that no one else would spot are reason for big celebrations.

So you find yourself pushing them on to that next milestone. But pushing soon becomes pushy. I can't help cheering Max on as I see him trying new things, but it's a fine line between cheering and pressuring. He has to learn for himself, and I have to be patient - every baby is different and develops at a different rate. He'll work all these things out and in the long run it'll make no difference if it took him a week or a month to learn something. But it's not easy. I'm a competitive guy and I really have to fight the urge to compare him to other babies we know around the same age.

It's hard to know what type of parent to be. I really don't want to be a control freak hyper-dad, pushy and intense, watching every second, reading every book, telling everyone else the correct way to do things. But on the other hand, it's easy to be too relaxed: patient, trusting and open-minded can easily tip into just being sloppy and negligent. All you can do is be yourself I guess. I'm trying not to overthink it.

WHERE DOES THE TIME GO?

AT HOME ALL WEEK WITH SONYA AND MAX. I THOUGHT WE'D HAVE PLENTY OF TIME. I THOUGHT IT'D BE A SLOW, LAZY, RELAXING PACE. DAMN! WHAT HAPPENS? WALKS, FEEDS, CHANGES—THE DAYS FLY BY.

CAUGHT IN THE
ACT: LITTLE
ESCAPE ARTIST

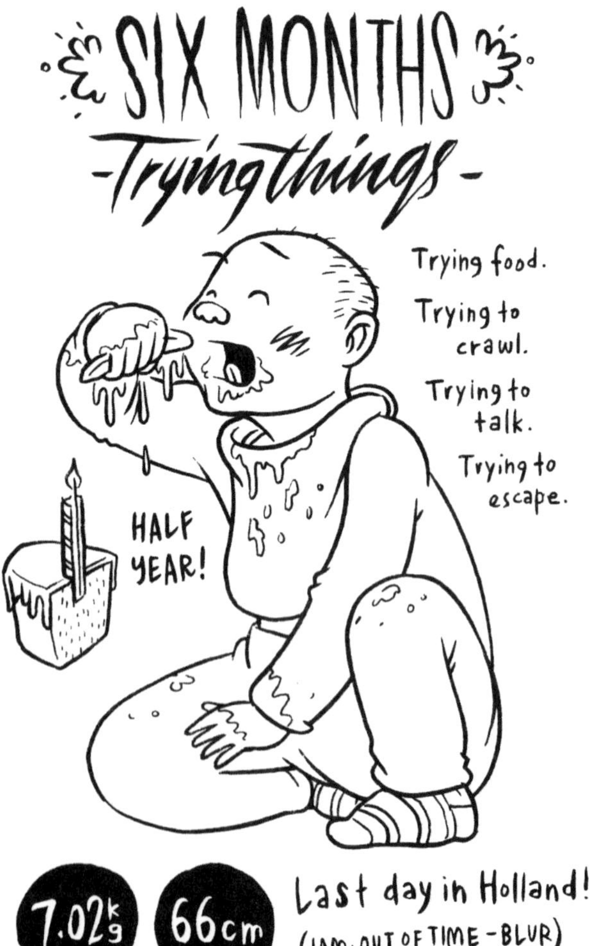
SIX MONTHS
-Trying things-
Trying food.
Trying to crawl.
Trying to talk.
Trying to escape.
HALF YEAR!
7.02 kg
66 cm
Last day in Holland!
(JAM: OUT OF TIME - BLUR)

Chapter Seven

Homecoming

April 2012

THE FLIGHT

ARE YOU SURE YOU
WANT TO HEAR THIS?

POOR LITTLE GUY PICKED UP A STOMACH BUG.
PROJECTILE VOMITED AND POOPED THE WHOLE
TWELVE HOURS. NO SLEEP, OBVIOUSLY...

This was the moment that I realised that no matter where we lived, life as a parent would be pretty similar. I'm walking the same boy in the same pram, I'm just wearing shorts instead of my winter coat.

When we were weighing up our move, we had it all wrong. We were thinking about our old versions of life in Wellington, Auckland, Amsterdam or Melbourne. Our idea of those cities was based on how they were when we were kids (we were 23 when we left New Zealand!). We judged them on criteria that just weren't relevant anymore – the price and quality of restaurants, the state of the local music scene, the nightlife, the travel opportunities. We loved Amsterdam because we could catch a train to Paris or Berlin for the weekend. We loved Melbourne because you could watch bands and drink outside in a singlet any night of the week.

None of that matters to us right now. So we're coming back to a home that suddenly feels like a whole new deal. We're in 'we've got a small baby' New Zealand. Choosing a new home now is more about being in walking distance to the park or the playcentre, than our regular pub or favourite cheap eats. It's a new place, where school zones and safety matter.

But it's not New Zealand that has changed, it's us.

KIWI FAMILY,
WAIHI BEACH

WHITE PINE BUSH,
HAWKES BAY

SITTING UP BY
HIMSELF AT
GREAT-GRANMA'S

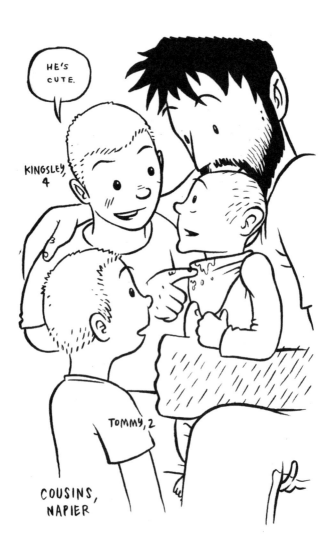

MAX IS EXPLORING,
KINGSLEY IS PICKING UP PHRASES

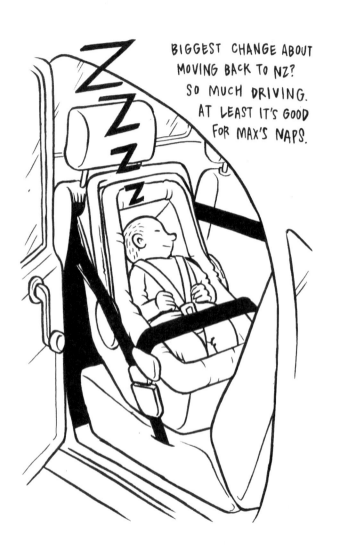

MAX THINKS AMOS IS FUNNY.
BIG HEARTY LAUGHS NOW.

Max "Two Teeth" Morris

(SECOND TIME: NO DRAMAS. THANK GOD.)

MAX MEETS
HIS GROOT-OPA,
TAURANGA

Introducing Max to all our relatives who hadn't met him yet made coming home make a lot of sense.

It was so amazing and fulfilling to see the joy Max brought to both our parents and our wider families. We realised it's something that's bigger than you – a baby means so much to the whole family, especially your own parents. Both mine and Sonya's parents are so gushy, they love Max so much. To be able to bring that excitement and joy back into our families' lives was huge – for them to be able to come for the weekend, to drop by, to have Christmases and birthdays together is big.

Having Max has made me appreciate my own parents a lot more too. After a long time away, both Sonya and I are appreciating and enjoying the benefits of wider family support. We had a great network of friends in Amsterdam, but nothing can match family.

I still think it's valuable to forge ahead, find your own path and make your own life away from what you know. I'm glad we did that and imagine I will encourage Max to do that one day, but in moving home again I'm also reminded there is value in being part of something bigger, of belonging, of sharing the good moments with the ones you love.

SEVEN MONTHS

DA DA DA DA!

So Max has been homeless for a month - living on the road, new people and new places everyday.

His routine is totally screwed.

But he's been great. Happy, curious, adaptable.

(LATEST TRICK: LOVES TO SIT IN OMA'S LAUNDRY BASKET)

But we're all still really really looking forward to settling down.

NO IDEA OF WEIGHT OR HEIGHT

Chapter Eight

FINDING OUR PLACE

May 2012

SWINGS BY THE
LAKE, HAMILTON

ENTHUSIASTIC EATER.
MAX TREMBLES
WITH EXCITEMENT
WHEN ITS FOOD TIME.

Hooray! This was the other big thing about moving home for us: a desperate desire for SPACE.

Our apartment in Amsterdam was so small. It was fine when it was just the two of us, cozy and comfortable, or gezillig as the Dutch say. But with three of us sharing one room, it was pretty tight. The thing is, babies don't just add an extra person to a house, they also bring with them an unimaginable amount of stuff. Mountains and mountains of stuff.

We stored the pram in the kitchen and it filled the room. To open the oven you had to move it into the lounge. We kept the baby bath in the shower and to have a shower you had to put it on the floor of the bathroom, so it too filled the room. When you got out of the shower you had to switch it back into the bath as you got out so that you had somewhere to stand. Max's change table was a dresser, the kitchen table became storage space. Babies take up a lot of room.

But it was the sleeping that most needed to change. With three of us in the room he wasn't sleeping through the night and neither were we.

We thought it was him waking us, but as we soon found out, it was us that started it. We were waking him with our snoring Turns out, he wanted his own room as much as we did.

SONYA AND MAX MEET
ME FOR LUNCH IN THE CITY.
MAX IS SO EXCITED,
SOAKING IT ALL IN.

HUGE PUKE IN HEAVY TRAFFIC.
EMERGENCY CAR-BONNET-
IN-SUPERMARKET-CARPARK
CLEAN-UP IN THE RAIN.

(TOO SOON FOR CHEESE)

Why do these things always happen at the worst possible moment? We're on our way to an important meeting, stressed and slightly lost, and Max heaves a huge cheese spew all over himself and the whole back seat of the car. This is not happening.

No matter how organised you are, how well planned your day is, or how perfectly you've packed the nappy bag, you realise you can never plan for everything. You simply can't be ready for what chance will throw at you. And by 'what chance will throw at you', I mean you can't be ready for spew to go everywhere at the worst possible time.

You have to learn to laugh. You know those moments of clarity? When you suddenly very clearly get a sense of where you are and what is going on? Why yes, I am standing in the rain in the carpark of Pak'n'Save Mt Albert changing baby clothes covered in cheese spew on a car bonnet. This is my life now.

Yes, it's one of those moments. This is actually happening.

Chapter Nine

June 2012

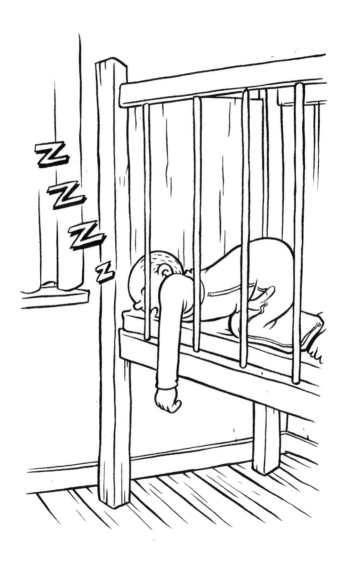

JEANS & FLANNEL.
x2

Do you want to bring up your son to be like you? The answer to that depends on whether you think you're a good person, a good man. And maybe depends on the answer to another question: Did you want to be like your dad? Are you turning out like him? I don't hear many guys say this, but in the end, I'm at peace with turning out like mine: he's a good man.

So I have to admit, I do want to bring Max up like me. I do want to see myself in him. I'll let him do his own thing, of course, find himself and all that (apart from choosing sports teams, I definitely reserve the right to influence those), but I hope that one day, after the inevitable 'you're so lame' teenage years, he comes around to a place where he decides that turning out like me would be ok.

What I don't want to do is to try and live my youth again through my son, to try and right my wrongs a second time over. I know that no matter how well he plays rugby, I'll never win that final against Rongotai in 1998. No matter how smooth and confident he is, I'll never be able to take back those hauntingly stupid things I said to girls. You can't change the past and I suspect you can't change the future that much either. We'll find out, I suppose. He'll turn out how he turns out. And quite possibly it'll be something like me, and my Dad, and his Dad.

Only hopefully a little bit better.

WHEN YOU'VE GOT TEETH YOU GOTTA BRUSH 'EM.

CRAWLING!
(WELL, PULLING HIMSELF
ALONG THE FLOOR)

SONYA MADE A
PLAYHOUSE OUT OF
MOVING BOXES

EVERY NOW & THEN,
FOR A SECOND THROUGH
HIS NEW TOOTHY GRIN,
I SEE A BOY NOT A BABY

5.45pm

I love bath time, and obviously so does Max.
He has enjoyed it since he was tiny, but recently,
newly upgraded to the big bath, he has stepped it
up a notch, breaking into a daily display of crazed
laughter and splashing.

Lying flat on his back, he starts off slow. A kick, a push
of the hand, a little shimmy. But a few minutes in, he
suddenly and drastically lets it all rip at once in a blast
of pure energy. Both arms and legs going full-bore in
a frantic rhythm, rocking from side to side like an out
of control spinning top. It's total commitment and
pure pleasure- he is splashing and laughing with a
manic squeal and a trance-like look in his eyes. It's an
explosion of movement and sound. Total joy.

It's freedom. I can see his daily frustration. He can't
quite crawl, can't quite coordinate himself, and I can
see he wants to so bad. In the bath he is weightless.
It's his chance to let loose, to unwind, to yell it all out.

9 MONTHS IN,
9 MONTHS OUT.

9 MONTHS
ON THE MOVE

Crawling well now. Always curious, exploring everywhere we go.

Total teeth: 6

Sleeping better.

Eating meat & bread and loving it.

Favourite song:
The Roots on
Yo Gabba Gabba

8.9kg
72cm

Chapter Ten

HE'S OFF

July 2012

Before Max, I always liked to think I'd be the type of parent that would let my kid take risks - climb trees, jump off fences, have the first crack at that ramp the neighbour kids built.

I think men want their kids to be confident and adventurous, to not grow up babied, always having every problem solved for them. But also, at some primal level - we want them to be tough. When I was a kid, I broke both arms, both legs, my hand, my collarbone, the works, and now I'm proud of that. Wouldn't change it if I could. I'm a big believer in learning to take knocks and I think in some areas we've gone too far in protecting kids from lesson-learning dangers. You can't hold their hands forever. Safety nets on trampolines? C'mon.

So I'd say I'm probably a fairly typical guy when it comes to believing in rough play, but damn it feels awful when I accidently hurt Max. Thankfully, I'm learning that that he's actually built quite tough - it's amazing to see the knocks he takes daily - but it's still really hard to see him upset.

What am I - invisible? It's amazing the ridiculous things perfect strangers will do and say to make a baby smile. Unsolicited baby talking, waving, weird faces, that's just a walk around the block. Random passersby lose all inhibition and gain a weird sense of entitlement when it comes to saying hello to a baby. They get sucked into the vortex of cuteness and become blind to the world around them. They'll totally forget you're there. You realise I can hear you right?

Imagine I walk into this shop without the pram. This grown man behind the counter, a perfect stranger who I assume is sane, spots me, another grown man who he does not know, pokes out his tongue, and says "helluuuoo little fellooooow" in a cootchie coo voice. He starts waving like a seven year old girl. "Who's a liddle cutey?" he coos, and wiggles his bum like he has a caterpillar in his pants. His eyes go cross eyed. His jazz hands sparkle.

See, that's really weird.

SUNNY
SATURDAY
MORNING
ON THE
PORCH

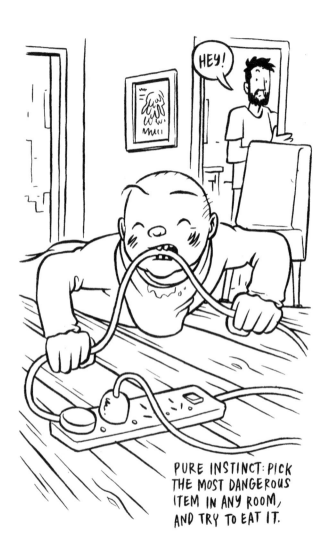

PURE INSTINCT: PICK
THE MOST DANGEROUS
ITEM IN ANY ROOM,
AND TRY TO EAT IT.

How do they do this? Babies have some inbuilt, radar, laser guidance system that allows them, in a split second, in any environment, to immediately identify the most dangerous object in the room and go straight for it. Are the scientists researching this?

If there is something that could electrocute them, glass that could smash, precious ornaments to break, cords to pull, anything that could bite them, impale them or flatten them, they'll go straight for it. Biting through a power cord is right up there on Max's current life goals, right behind pulling over the kitchen shelves and being eaten by a large dog. Put him down in a room for the first time and he'll spot the deathportunity in a second. Why does he always sit right on the edge of the top step with his back to the steps? How, when he reaches his hand into a drawer he can't see into, does he always manage to pull out a knife? I can't take my eyes off him! As a parent you get this future-vision where you're always seeing five minutes ahead, assuming the worst. Anything that can go wrong does, in your imagination.

Is it always like this? Is this the start of a lifetime of Max trying to touch what he's not supposed to touch? Wanting to go where he's not allowed to go? When can I stop worrying?

BABY DATE: MEETING
ESTHER, DUNCAN & MAHI

At this point not many of our friends have kids, so people are always trying to set us up with other couples they know with babies. "Oh you'll get along great", they'll say, and then here I am, as a grown man with a partner and child, going on blind friend dates. Just because we have a baby of the same age, you think we're going to get along? One thing in common! Would you set me up with someone who also has a green jersey?

But as it turns out, it's a pretty massive thing to have in common. It's a big thing to share, and it's really good to have people to share it with. When most of your friends don't really understand what's happening, having people from your planet who are also going through the same stuff is really valuable.

It's also really easy. I'm terrible at making friends, but with kids to talk about you're chatting away for ages and before you know it, you accidentally veer into regular human-being topics. It's just as well too - I foresee a future where I'll spend a lot of time in the company of a lot of strange characters I would never cross paths with if we didn't have a kid in the same class or sports team.

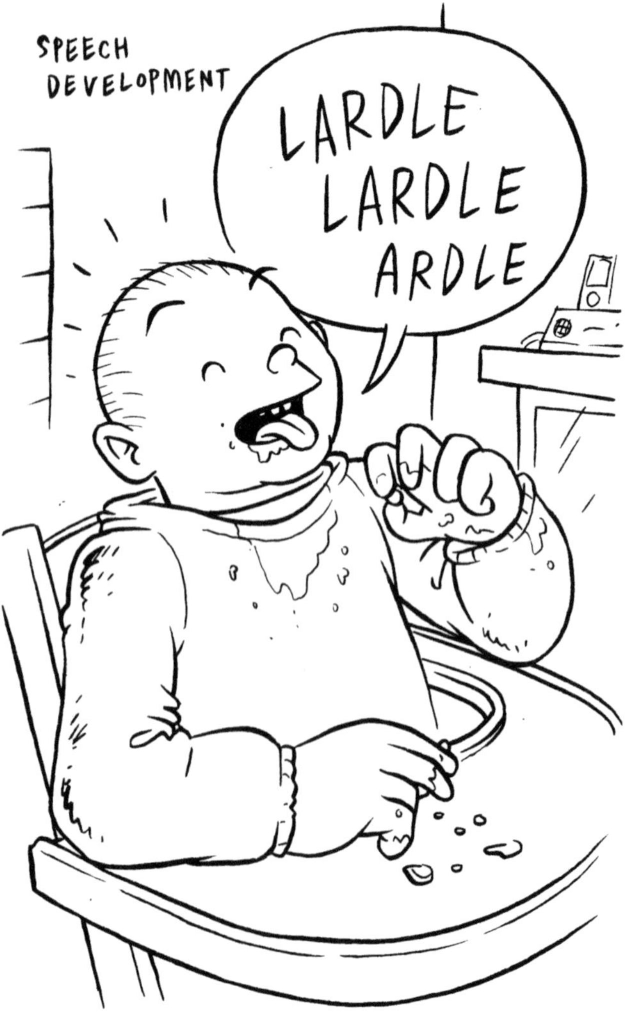
SPEECH DEVELOPMENT
LARDLE LARDLE ARDLE

DADA!
10 MONTHS
CRAWLING
CLIMBING
LOVES TO STAND
HAPPY
MIMICKING SOUNDS
9.3kg
73.5cm
MUSIC: ALPHABUTT
-KIMYA DAWSON

Chapter Eleven

ACTION

August 2012

DANCING AT GRANNY AND G-POP'S PLACE

When a baby is first born, it is usually placed straight away on its mother's chest. The touch and smell and sound of the mother's voice is supposed to cement an immediate bond between the child and mother, as if living inside her for nine months hadn't done it already. And even if the bond doesn't form instantly, the months ahead of feeding and soothing ensure that the child quickly learns to love its mother like its life depends on it. Because it does.

But for dads, the bond is something that takes a little longer to form. Let's face it, without milk jugs on your torso, to the newborn baby, you're the useless one. Sure, you have a role - support, lots of nappy changes, long walks and all that - but to the baby it's not so obvious what purpose you serve. Get out of my way, you're boob-blocking me, hairy man!

By now I've finally managed to win Max over. These days he cries when I leave for work each morning, banging on the door with sad little fists, and I have to admit that comes with mixed emotions. It's hard to hear him upset, but I'd be lying if I said there wasn't a part of me that is glad to know that he cares.

BIG BOYS
GET DIRTY
KNEES

ULTIMATE QUEST III:
CLIMB INSIDE THE
DISHWASHER

NOT ASLEEP.

Baby Bonnie seems so tiny and fragile in my arms, so impossibly small and perfect. Luke and Kelly look both tired and glowing at the same time. It makes me feel like we've come so far, and it makes 10 month old Max suddenly look so big.

We see so much of ourselves from just a few months earlier. When we arrived Luke had lined up the tea cups ready to be poured, just like I used to do. The sugar is in the bowl, the cake is sliced up ready to be served. They've got the baby visit routine down to perfection and chatting to them, so many of the stories, questions and emotions are exactly what we'd talked about to our visitors in those first months back in Amsterdam.

I have a clear memory from when I was eight: my neighbour Kirk on the morning of his first day at intermediate, heading off down our street in his new uniform. He was the first of our group to go there, to wear a uniform, and I remember thinking how big he looked, and feeling that he had now grown up. He looked like a man. He would have been 10.

Today it's 10 month old Max feeling huge. I'm sure we'll look back at photos of him at that age and he'll be tiny. And right now I feel really old, but at least someday we'll look at photos of now and marvel at how young we all look.

FAMILY SLEEP-INS
AREN'T WORKING

Chapter Twelve

BIG BOY

September 2012

When they're small, you're always talking to them, but you have no idea of how much of it, if any, is really sinking in. While I chat away to Max, I sometimes feel like a Charlie Brown teacher. Womp womp wah wah womp. I might as well be reciting Japanese legal contracts. If I'm smiling, he's smiling, if I'm serious, he's serious.

It's your tone and presence they're responding to. They understand the intention behind what you're saying, there is some communication back and forth, but it's more about body language than words. It's hard to know at what point they start to actually understand you.

So it was an amazing feeling when Max started to respond to specific words. It felt like a curtain that was blocking us understanding each other had finally been lifted. Now, I say dance and he dances and it's the happiest dance I've ever seen. It's a dance about more than loving the music — it's a dance about connecting.

FAMILY SWIMMING,
WAIWERA

I FEEL LIKE WE'RE MISSING SOMEONE
DAY BABYSITTER: FIRST TIME WE'VE GONE TO THE MOVIES IN A YEAR.

TERRIFIED OF
VACUUM CLEANER

SHARING.

LEARNING TO PASS

THE CAKE

The first birthday is all about the parents. It's a milestone, a clear mark in the sand. A time when you're allowed to stand back, take a breath and enjoy the feeling that you haven't stuffed it up yet. So far so good!

So when it came to how to commemorate such an important moment, one option jumped out for both Sonya and I - the classic Australian Women's Weekly cake book. Every Kiwi around my age grew up with this book. As kids we'd spend hours and hours flicking through and making plans for what we were going to ask for, months and sometimes years in advance. I have fond memories of the pirate, the race track, the train. For Sonya, it was the swimming pool, the piano, and the cat cakes. The book holds a lot of sentimental value for both of us.

So we tracked it down and flicked through it once again. Like kids we ummed and aahed, but we finally settled on the exact same design my mum made for me on my first birthday - the teddy bear. Sonya made it beautifully. Full circle.

FAMILY ALBUM

First day

A family

So small

Grumpy Max

Look at this guy!

christmas

Dutchies

Home Again

Max with his cousins and Uncle Guy

Crawling!

Washing watcher

Food is fun

Growing Up

Learning to walk

First of all, thanks to Sally, Ande and Kitki at Beatnik for transforming this from a pile of sketchbooks to the book you hold now. And thanks to Rachel and Brynne for helping edit the text.

My work partners - Ebba in Amsterdam, Simone in Auckland- have both been generous in their patience, advice and support. Thank you. Mark, Eric, Andy, and W+k Amsterdam and DDB Auckland more generally: thanks for being understanding and supportive and allowing me the room to have creative projects outside of work as well.

I'm grateful also to all our family and friends who've let me draw them without complaint and given their thoughts and support along the way, both with this book and our parenting in general. Thanks for being Max fans with us.

But biggest thanks go to Sonya who has supported and encouraged and critiqued and laughed with me throughout. Thank you for your patience. Thank you having faith in me. Thanks for letting me get out of all those nappy changes while I was in the middle of a drawing.

And Max, if you're reading this in the future sometime, thank you too. I hope you enjoy it.

Toby Morris is an illustrator,
designer and art director
recently returned to New Zealand
after nine years abroad.

Max Morris is one year old.
He likes to eat bananas.